T0209300

ONLINE FINITE ELEMENT ANALYSIS COURSE

DR. JAMES A. MANDEL, P.E.

ONLINE FINITE ELEMENT ANALYSIS COURSE

iUniverse books may be ordered through booksellers or by contacting:

iUniverse
1663 Liberty Drive
Bloomington, IN 47403
www.iuniverse.com
844-349-9409

Because of the dynamic nature of the Internet, any web addresses or links contained in this book may have changed since publication and may no longer be valid. The views expressed in this work are solely those of the author and do not necessarily reflect the views of the publisher, and the publisher hereby disclaims any responsibility for them.

Any people depicted in stock imagery provided by Getty Images are models, and such images are being used for illustrative purposes only.
Certain stock imagery © Getty Images.

ISBN: 978-1-6632-4378-2 (sc)
ISBN: 978-1-6632-4380-5 (hc)
ISBN: 978-1-6632-4379-9 (e)

Library of Congress Control Number: 2022915130

Print information available on the last page.

iUniverse rev. date: 08/24/2022

Dedicated to my wife Carolyn

INTRODUCTION TO THE FINITE ELEMENT JAM 3/14/14

ANALYSIS ON-LINE COURSE

A - OBJECTIVES OF THE COURSE

There are several objectives in this course. These include teaching the history, basic principles, and the theory of finite element analysis. The students will also be taught to intelligently use the finite element analysis software, ANSYS. The students will also be introduced to applications of finite element analysis to "real world" applications. These applications include, but are not limited to, analysis of thin shells, fracture mechanics, analysis of reinforced beams and columns, stress analysis, earthquake analysis of structures, buckling, seepage under a dam, and a medical example, registration of MRI and PET scans.

Along with each of these example applications, a brief lecture is given to teach the students the basic principles of these areas. Some of these examples come from my personal work experiences and research. Technical publications authored by me and persons instrumental in the development of the finite element method are used as examples in this course.

Another primary objective of this course is to teach the students how to work as engineers. To accomplish this they will be taught how to use deductive reasoning and have "scale" when solving a "real" engineering problem. This will be accomplished through material taught in the course and by teaching them how, as a required part of their homework assignments, to write engineering reports. Each student is required to submit a proposal for a semester project using finite element analysis, have it approved, and submit the results in the form of an engineering report. Each student will have a different project.

B - HOW THE FINITE ELEMENT ANALYSIS SOFTWARE ANSYS WILL BE USED

ANSYS is a widely used multiple purpose finite element analysis software. Input data to this program is entered in two basic ways, a word processing file NOTEPAD and a guided user interface (GUI). In this course, NOTEPAD files are used to input data for the following reasons.

Finite element analysis, if the necessary checks are made, yields an exact solution to an approximate problem. Whether this approximate solution is the same as the solution of the "real" problem depends of the skill of the engineer to construct a engineering model and input that model into ANSYS. Using NOTEPAD for input has advantages in both practical engineering and teaching. When defining the input data this way, the user has a record of the logic used to construct a proper engineering model, an easy way to finding and correcting errors, as well as having a detailed permanent record of the input data. For these reasons NOTEPAD files will be used in this course.

HOW THE COURSE MATERIAL WAS DEVELOPED

The lectures (sessions), for this course were recorded using a document camera and sound recording equipment. All material that was shown with the document camera was handed to the students prior to the actual session. This material as well as the homework assignments and solutions, the final exam, and other information are organized into the following computer files placed in folders within the folder "E-BOOK".

CONTENTS OF THE E - BOOK

1. For each session the following files will be in a folder for that session:
   a. All handout material for that session
   b. NOTEPAD files for the examples used in the handout material for that session
2. Additional folders are included for:
   a. Introduction and objective of the course
      b. Summary of the material covered in each session
      c. Other handouts
   d. Homework assignments

e. Syllabus

f. Final exam

g. Grading

h. Typical Student Project Reports

    i. Resume – Dr. James A. Mandel PE

    j. Student evaluation and comments

    k. Addendum

In the recorded session, there are small errors such as the wrong word used. In the addendum folder, these errors are corrected. Note the time in the session where these errors occurred is included.

To access the On – Line Course, install the thumb in an USB port. Figure 1 will appear on the monitor.

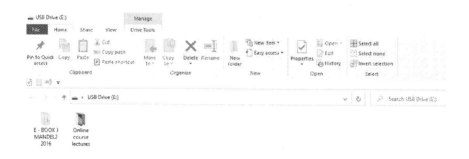

Figure 1

To view an on – line lecture, double click on Online course lectures. The following figure will appear on the monitor.

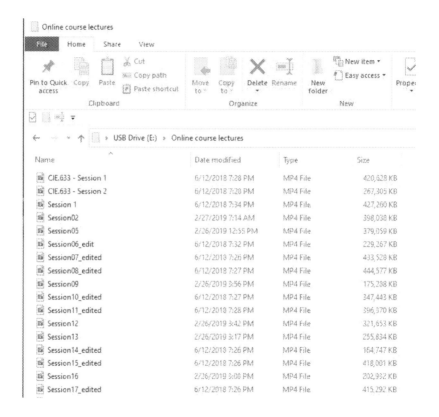

Note: The list of Online course lectures continues until session 28.

Figure 2

If you double click on a session, that lecture will appear on the monitor. You will see and hear me lecturing. On the bottom left of the screen, a time line and volume control icons will appear. On the bottom right of the screen are three icons.

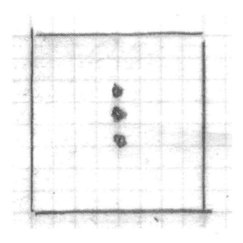

Figure 3 – Exit Full Screen

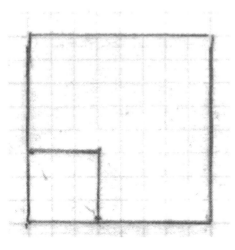

Figure 4 – Return to Figure 1

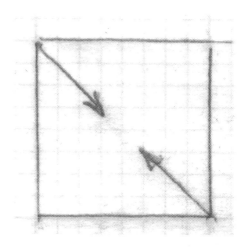

Figure 5 – Exit Full Screen

If the student passes an advanced credit exam and pays the tuition, graduate credit is generally awarded.

TO VIEW E – BOOK

Insert Thumb drive in an USB Port. Figure 1 will appear on the monitor.

Figure 1

ONLINE FINITE ELEMENT ANALYSIS COURSE

Double click on E – Book J

MANDEL2

2016

The following figure will appear on the monitor.

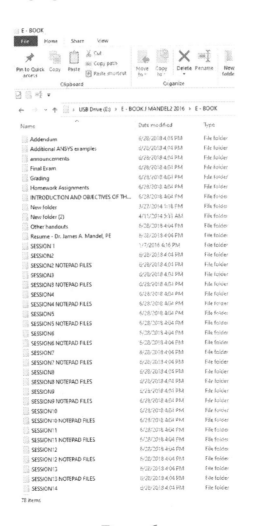

Figure 6

Note the sessions in figure 6 continue until Summary of material covered in E.... To see details in a session, double click on that session. Details of the sessions are given in the <u>contents of the e – book section</u> on page 3.

SUMMARY OF MATERIAL COVERED IN EACH SESSION

SESSION 1

In session 1 an introduction to Finite Element Analysis was presented. The first part of this review covered the history of structural analysis from the development of the energy theorems until matrix method of structures. The finite element method was developed by Ray Clough while he was working at Boeing Aircraft. He was trying to extend the matrix method of structures to include continuum material. After he developed the finite element method he realized that the matrix method of structures was special case of the finite element method. The first published paper on the finite element was in 1960. The first finite element was similar to the constant strain triangle element. Ray Clough went to the University of California at Berkeley. The University of

California at Berkeley became the center of finite element development. People from all over the world came to Berkeley to study the finite element method. The handout, "The finite element method friend or foe" reviews the steps of the finite element method. In step 1, a finite element model is assumed. The model consists of finite elements connected together at nodes along the boundaries of the finite elements. Loads and supports are also located at nodal points. This is a key step in that an approximate problem is assumed. The finite element method gives an exact solution to this approximate problem. The other steps in the finite element method are also reviewed.

To help explain the steps in the finite element method, the constant strain triangle element is used as an example. The students are expected to study this handout and learn the fundamentals of the finite element method

SESSION 2

In this session the steps in a finite element method are reviewed. These steps are covered in the handout "The finite element method friend or foe" This handout is completed in this session. Building codes are discussed. The first building code by Hammurabi in 2200 B.C. is presented. Modern building codes are also discussed. The students are expected to study this material and start on the first homework problem. This problem consists of a deep cantilever beam with two constant strain triangular finite elements. This problem is to be solved in closed form.

SESSION 3

In session 3, the students are shown how to assemble the element stiffness matrices to compute the global stiffness matrix for the entire domain of the problem. The boundary conditions and loads are applied and the resulting equations are solved for the nodal displacements. At this point the students can solve the first homework problem. In this session, the software ANSYS is also presented. The fundamentals of using this software are reviewed. The students are expected to study this material. Session 4 will be held in a computer laboratory where the students can solve the first homework problem using ANSYS and compare the results with their long and solution.

SESSION 4

Session 4 is held in a computer laboratory. The student learn to use ANSYS software using NOTEPAD files as input. Basic ANSYS commands are explained. Note ANSYS instruction will continue throughout the course.

SESSION 5

In a session 5, the theory of finite element analysis is reviewed. The method of virtual work is used to derive integrals to calculate the element stiffness matrix and the equivalent nodal loads for a temperature loading, a body force, and a distributed load along the side of an element. The student is expected to review the theory of finite element analysis and apply the calculation of elements stiffness matrix and equivalent nodal loads to the constant strain triangular element.

SESSION 6

In session 6, a complete derivation of the constant strain triangular element is presented in closed form. The virtual work derivation for an element stiffness matrix and equivalent nodal loads is reviewed. The case of an elastic plate in tension with a hole is discussed and assigned as a homework problem. The properties of steel are discussed. The difference between an elastic analysis and an elastic – plastic analysis is presented. The students are expected to review the finite element analysis theory and start on the homework problem. The analyses for this problem are to be done with ANSYS. Several meshes are to be used. Extrapolation to the limit is to be used to check for convergence of the stress concentration factor at the hole. This result is to be checked with the theoretical value.

SESSION 7

In sessions 7, natural coordinate systems are introduced. The conformal map between a parent and child element is explained. Convergence criteria for finite elements as well as the patch test are discussed. The elastic plate with a hole homework problem assignment problem is discussed. An ANSYS finite element solution for a simply supported plate with a uniform loading is also presented. The students are expected to study this material and to continue working on the elastic plate with a hole homework problem.

SESSION 8

In session 8, improved finite elements with natural coordinate systems are presented. The history and practice of linear elastic fracture mechanics is also presented. The students are expected to study this material.

SESSION 9

In session 9, a finite element analysis solution using ANSYS of a centrally cracked plate in tension is presented. The students are shown in detail how to solve this problem for the opening and sliding mode stress intensity factors. A finite element analysis solution using ANSYS for a centrally cracked plate in tension with a riveted stiffener is also presented. A homework problem of a centrally cracked plate in tension with a riveted stiffener is assigned. The solution to this homework problem is to be in the form of an engineering report.

SESSION 10

In session 10, a detailed example of an engineering report is presented. Thee homework problem, presented in session 9 is discussed. The students are expected to study the concepts of linearly elastic fracture mechanics and start on the homework problem.

SESSION 11

In session 11, the theory for seepage under a dam is presented. This problem is treated like a field problem so the stiffness matrix for the finite element is computed by minimizing the functional relationship associated with the partial differential equation for the seepage problem (LaPlaces Equation). A finite element analysis solution for seepage under a dam is obtained using ANSYS. The problem is solved as a steady state heat transfer problem as the partial differential equations for the seepage and heat transfer problems are both LaPlaces equation.

SESSION 12

In session 12, the seepage under a dam topic was finished. A finite element analysis solution using ANSYS of a reinforced concrete beam was presented. Ultimate Strength Design of concrete beams was reviewed. The differences between these two methods of analysis were discussed. The students are expected to study this material and to also study the characteristics of SOLID65, the concrete element in ANSYS.

SESSION 13

In session13, there was further discussion on reinforced concrete analysis using ANSYS. Service load design of reinforced concrete was reviewed and compared to finite element analysis of reinforced concrete using ANSYS. Nonlinear analysis using finite element analysis was discussed. The students are expected to study this material. Their proposals for a project for this course are due next week.

SESSION 14

In session 14, the class was devoted to using ANSYS for linear and nonlinear problems. Techniques for finding and correcting errors in NOTEPAD input files were discussed.

SESSION 15

In session15, the solution for the centrally cracked plate with a riveted stiffener homework problem was discussed. Meshing for this problem was discussed in detail. Two dimensional node to node interface elements were introduced. Singular quarter point cracktip elements were also introduced.

SESSION 16

In session 16, a three dimensional node to node interface element was discussed. Meshing was also discussed. An outline for an engineering report was presented again since their course projects reports must be in the form of an engineering report. The students are expected to study this material and work on their course projects.

SESSION 17

In session 17, interface elements and quarter point crack-tip elements in a material on the interface between two materials were reviewed. Thin shell theory was presented. A spherical shell was analyzed for membrane and bending stresses using ANSYS The results were shown to agree closely with a theoretical solution. A spherical shell approximately the size of the Manley Field House was also analyzed using ANSYS. The students were expected to study this material and work on their projects. NOTEPAD files were given to the students so they can run the examples presented in class in ANSYS.

SESSION 18

In session 18, examples of finite element analysis of spherical and cylindrical thin shells using NSYS were presented. An example of constructing a finite element mesh around a reinforcing bar in concrete was also presented.

SESSION 19

In session 19, SHELL63, an ANSYS finite element for plate and shells was reviewed. The stresses due to dead load in a barrel shell roof, similar to the War Memorial Auditorium in Syracuse, N.Y., were computed using ANSYS. SHELL41, an ANSYS membrane element, and LINK10, an ANSYS cable element, were introduced. Using these two finite elements, the stresses in a portion of the Carrier Dome at Syracuse University were computed using ANSYS.

An introduction to fiber reinforced concrete, a chopped fiber composite, was presented. Experimental research and micromechanical finite element analysis of fiber reinforced concrete was presented. This work was funded by the National Science Foundation. The work was done by myself and my students.

SESSION 20

In session 20, the unit on micromechanical finite element analysis of fiber reinforced concrete was completed. Barsoum's quarter point crack-tip element and a zero thickness quarter point finite element used to model a crack tip on the interface between two materials, developed by Tarazi and Mandel, were discussed.

SESSION 21

Progress reports on the student's projects were collected. They will be corrected and returned to the students at the next class. Some of the difficulties that students are having will be shared with entire class for educational purposes. EGEN, an ANSYS command to generate element data was discussed. This command is useful for inputting the reinforcing in concrete beams and columns, the subject area of several student projects. A detailed derivation of the isoparametric quadratic quadrilateral element (PLANE82 in ANSYS) was presented. The students are expected to study this material and work on their projects.

SESSION 22

In session 22, dynamic analysis of structure-soil-rock systems was discussed. An example to compute the natural frequencies and dynamic response of a typical nuclear reactor building was presented. This work was done at Syracuse University. It was funded research.

SESSION 23

In session 23, a finite element technique for a simplified dynamic analysis of a typical nuclear reactor building was presented. Analysis of a reinforced concrete beam was also presented. An example of a method to place a crack in a finite element model of a reinforced concrete beam was discussed. The students are expected to study this material and work on their projects.

SESSION 24

A technique using Finite Element Analysis with ANSYS to register (combine) a MRI and PET scan of a ladies breast is presented. This technique was based on an analogy between the registration problem and a 3D steady state heat transfer problem. This technique was used successfully in breast cancer patient studies. Note this work was done by me for the radiology department of the New York Upstate Medical University. The PhD student I co-advised on this project won the "All University Prize for PhD Dissertation and Study" at Syracuse University in 2006.

SESSION 25

A transient dynamic analysis of a spring – damper system was presented. A nonlinear analysis was done of an A36 grade steel plate with a hole in tension. A comparison of linear and nonlinear analyses of this problem was presented.

Sample questions for a final exam were discussed. Note these questions were presented to give the students an example of what the final exam would be like. Note the students are expected to learn all of the material in the course. This includes finite element analysis theory, ANSYS software, and the theory and finite element analysis of all the examples presented in this course.

SESSION 26

In session 26, finite element examples of buckling and slope stability were presented. St. Venant's principle was discussed and applied to the finite element analysis of the loading of a reinforced concrete column. The students are expected to study this material, work on their projects and review for the final exam.

SESSION 27

In session 27, the MIT assumed stress hybrid finite element was presented. A review for the finite element was started.

SESSION 28

In session 28, the last session, the review for the final exam was completed. A reinforced concrete beam, in which the coefficients of linear expansion for the concrete and the reinforcing were different, was analyzed for a temperature loading. The purpose of this example is to alert the students to the potentially large stresses that can occur for this situation. Substructuring, a finite element analysis technique that can be used when the number of nodes and elements is too large, was explained.

There are several objectives in this book. These include teaching the history, basic principles, and the theory of finite element analysis. The students will be introduced to applications of finite element analysis to "real world" applications. These applications include, but are not limited to, analysis of thin shells, fracture mechanics, analysis of reinforced beams and columns, stress analysis, earthquake analysis of structures, buckling, seepage under a dam, and a medical example, registration of MRI and PET scans.

Some of these examples come from my own personal work experiences and research. Technical publications authored by me and persons instrumental in the development of the finite element method are also used as examples in this course.

Another goal of this book is to teach the students how to work as engineers. To accomplish this they will be taught how to use deductive reasoning and have "scale" when solving a "real" engineering problem. This will be accomplished through material taught in the course and by teaching them how to write engineering reports.

The finite element software taught in this book is ANSYS. ANSYS is a widely used multiple purpose finite element analysis software. Input data to ANSYS can be done in two ways, either with a NOTEPAD file or a guided user interface (GUI). The guided user interface provides windows for the input data. In this book, NOTEPAD files are used for the following reasons.

The initial step in the construction of a NOTEPAD file is construct a "flow diagram" for analysis of the problem. The steps in the flow diagram become ANSYS commands in a NOTEPAD file. The NOTEPAD file is a detailed permanent record of the input data and your logic.

If you are later solving a similar problem, the NOTEPAD file provides an excellent starting point.

DR. JAMES A. MANDEL, P.E.

The NOTEPAD file provides an easy way to finding and correcting errors. The ANSYS command "finish" can be placed anywhere in NOTEPAD file. When executing the ANSYS NOTEPAD file, it stops when it comes to a "finish" command. The results up to that point can then be checked. It a good idea to first solve The problem is your engineering model input with your NOTEPAD input file. Whether this approximate solution is the same as the solution of the "real" problem depends on the is also advised to first solve a similar problem of known solution. This provides an additional vital check.

Finite element analysis gives the exact solution to an approximate problem. skill of the engineer. To use the finite element analysis method, one must know both the finite element analysis and the technical area of the problem. If you don't, you can get the right answer to the wrong problem.

This book is based on a graduate finite element course I taught at Syracuse University. The lectures for this course were recorded using a document camera and sound recording equipment. All material that was shown with the document camera was organized into files in what I called an "E-BOOK".

The first step in finite element analysis is to define an engineering model for your problem. Consider defining a model for a bridge or building. A connection in a bridge or building is very complicated. It has many bolts. A finite model that includes every bolt is not feasible. Engineers from their experience must know which variables to include in their finite element model.

A. REVIEW OF TECHNICAL AREAS

Technical areas will now be reviewed make sure you have a satisfactory background in engineering and science to understand this book.

What is the difference between a closed form solution and a numerical solution? In a closed form solution, the answer is given in the form of equations. This is the best possible scenario. These equations show the effect of the variables on the solution. A parametric study of the effect of the variables can lead to a better design.

There are two kinds of nonlinearities, material and geometric. Material nonlinearities occur when a material yields. Geometric nonlinearities occur when the displacements are not small compared to the dimensions of the structure.

In most Mechanics of Materials courses, the flexure formula $\sigma = M\, y/I$ is derived. These assumptions made are in the derivation.

1. Plane Sections before bending are plane after bending.
2. The deflections of the beam are much less than the length and depth of the beam.
3. The depth of the beam is much less than the length of the beam.
4. The material of the beams in the elastic range (Hookean material).

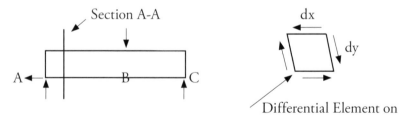

Figure 7 – <u>Simply Supported Beam</u> Section A-A

The first assumption does not consider displacements due to shear on section A-A. If the displacements due to both moment and shear are included, Section A-A will be curved, not plane.

A structure where all of the external and internal forces moments can be determined with Newton's laws is said to be statically determinate. The simply supported beam in Figure 1.1 is statically determinate. If an additional support is added at point B, an additional equation is needed. The displacement at point B is zero. This equation is called a compatibility equation. The structure is now statically indeterminate. A famous civil engineer, Hardy Cross's definition of compatibility is. "If it doesn't pull apart, it sticks together".

Most engineering problems are expressed in the form of a partial differential equation. These equations, in general, cannot be solved unless the boundaries are either circular or go to zero or infinity. Thus most problems must be solved numerically.

Unfortunately numerical solutions are only for the dimensions used. They do not show the effect of the variables on the solution.

Step 1 in a numerical solution is to make an engineering estimate of the final solution. This estimate is then solved numerically. Check to see if the solution is both safe and economical. If it is celebrate, you have solution to the problem. If the solution is not both safe and economical, go back to step 1. A good experienced engineer can estimate the final solution within 10%.

The most widely used method to get a numerical solution is the finite element method. It gets the exact solution to an approximate problem. Prior to the finite element method, the finite difference method was used. It gets an approximate answer to the exact solution.

There are many design specifications. Some of these are the American Association of State Highway and Transportation Officials, AASHTO, for the design of bridges, AREA for the design of railroad bridges, The American Concrete Institute, ACI code, the American Institute of Steel Construction,

AISC code for steel structures, and many other building codes. Codes are the law and they also provide a guide to design. Codes specify design loads and allowable stresses.

In the 1960's, Interstate Route was built. It went through downtown Syracuse, N.Y. The bridges girders are four to five feet deep. The girder spans are approximately eighty feet. The allowable stresses in the 1953 Standard Specifications for Highway Bridges for A36 steel are 20000 psi for bending and 13500 psi for shear. These girders were designed for moment and checked for shear.

The 1953 Standard Specifications for Highway Bridges is a book that is 6 inch by 9 inch. It is approximately 3/4 of an inch thick.

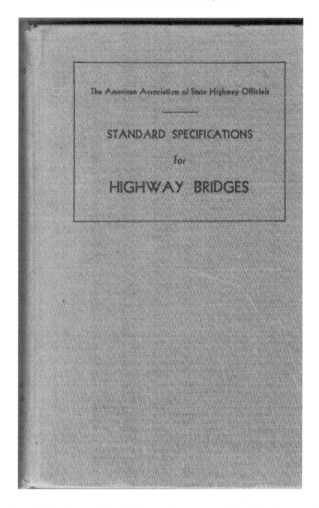

Figure 8 -1953 Standard Specifications for Highway Bridges

It is an excellent guide for the design. Current AASHTO specifications are in several loose leaf binders. If one designed a bridge with both specifications, the designs would be very close to each other. "A bridge does not know what specifications were used in the design, it only knows whether to fail or not".

Based on the final design, a set of design drawings are made. They are stamped by a Registered Professional Engineer. If there was a printing error in the design specifications on the unsafe side and the bridge failed, who is responsible? The engineer is responsible. He or she stamped the design drawings. The penalty could be a fine or loss of license.

The first building code was written in 2020 BC by the King of Babylonia, Hammurabi. The penalty for building collapse was much more severe then.

When I was in school and in my early days as an engineer, there were no calculators. You might say "oh my goodness you were really at a disadvantage". When actually, there were advantages. Because there were no computers, there was no software to solve problems. I had to do it "longhand". I had to do all the steps that would be done in the software. This process showed how the design variables affected the solution. This experience is useful when developing a finite element model. When I was a young engineer, I had a slide rule.

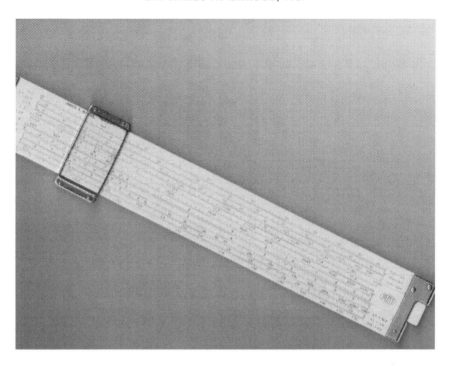

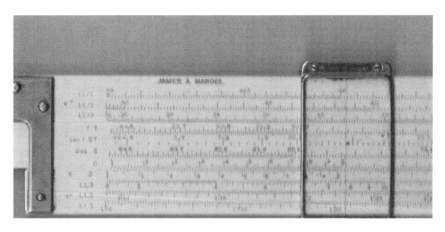

Figure 10 – <u>My Slide Rule</u>

It was two pieces of wood and a cursor. I could get the
first three digits of the answer when I multiplied, divided, got

a trig function, a square root, and many other mathematical operations. I had to calculate the power of 10 in my head.

Three significant digits are enough. We don't know the loads or material properties more accurately than three significant digits. In design specifications, loads and allowable stresses are also only given to three significant digits. If one shows too many digit of accuracy, their work will suspect.

When scientific calculators became available, there were two brands, Hewlett-Packard and Texas Instruments. Some students taking an exam would write down all the digits showing on their calculators. I can tell you what brand calculator they had because the Hewlett-Packard showed ten digits and the Texas Instrument calculator showed eight digits. I am not saying this to be funny. When you show all of the digits in a report, you will be viewed as inexperienced. Design calculations are only accurate to three significant digits.

B. THE HISTORY OF STRUCTURAL ANALYSIS

The modern period of structural analysis began in 1857. Mathematicians including Maxwell, Betti, and Castigliano. developed conservation of energy theorems to analyze statically indeterminate structure. Their solutions required solving a set of linear simultaneous equation. If the structure was large this could lead to a large number of equations.

Solving ten simultaneous linear equations requires 10^3 /3 = 333 arithmetic operations. Unfortunately, if an error is made, all arithmetic operations after that are wrong. You have to start over.

In 1936, Hardy Cross invented a numerical process for the analysis of statically indeterminate structures. His invention led the way to the design and construction of statically indeterminate structures all over the world.

With the coming of the computer age, simultaneous linear equations could be solved. Matrix Methods of Structural Analysis was developed. The equations are put into matrices for easier computer analysis. The structural model could include only discrete members such as beams and columns. Continuous structural elements such as floors, walls, and exterior panels could not be included in the structural model.

An engineer, Ray Clough, was working at Boeing Aircraft Company. He wanted to extend the Matrix Methods of Structural Analysis to include continuous elements such as the skin of an aircraft. He soon realized the Matrix Methods of Structural Analysis was only a one subset of the finite element method. In 1960, Ray Clough published the first paper on the Finite Element Method "The Finite Element Method in Plane Stress Analysis, 2nd Conference on Electric Computation, Pittsburgh, Pa (1960)". His element was a quadrilateral element. If you collapsed one side of that quadrilateral element, the result is the constant strain triangle element.

The software that is selected for this on line course is ANSYS. It is one of the most widely used finite element software. A multitude of different types of problems can be solved with ANSYS. In the following chapters, "real world" applications from my experience and from other sources will be presented.

C. STEPS IN THE FINITE ELEMENT METHOD

will now be presented. The constant strain triangle element shown below will be used in this example. It is a two dimensional element.

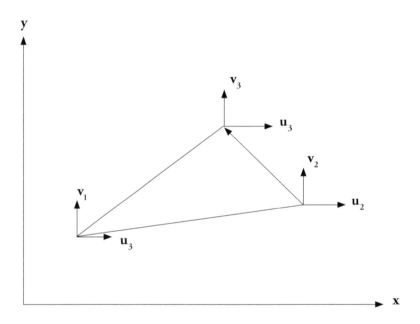

Figure 11 – <u>Constant Strain Triangle Element</u>

Some of the steps are "key steps". They require engineering judgement. The first step is to divide the domain of the problem into finite elements. The finite element mesh should not be uniform. There are more elements are in the important regions of the problem. A key assumption is now made, How do the displacements vary across the domain of a finite element.

$$u = \alpha_1 + \alpha_2 x + \alpha_3 y$$
$$v = \alpha_4 + \alpha_5 x + \alpha_6 y$$

$\alpha_1, \alpha_2, \alpha_3, \alpha_4, \alpha_5,$ and α_6 are called generalized coordinates. They are constants that change from element to element.

The next step is to compute the stiffness matrix for each finite element. Then we assemble them to get a stiffness matrix for the entire domain of the problem. The boundary condition s and loads are applied. This results in a set of simultaneous linear equations.

$$[K] \, [q] = [p]$$

Where:

[K] is the stiffness matrix

[q] is a matrix of nodal displacements

[p] is a matrix of nodal loads

The equations are solved for the nodal displacements. The element stresses are computed using back substitution.

The last step is a "key step". The solution is checked for convergence.

Because the constant strain triangle is an element of constant strain and stress is proportional to strain, each element is an island of constant stress. Changes of stress are modeled by changes from element to element.

There are many ways to get the wrong answer.

1. Wrong element type
2. Element size too large or too small.
3. If the internal angles of an element are too small.
4. Some elements have poor convergence properties.

There are two types of errors.

Discretization Errors – Differences between real structure and the finite element solution. If the finite elements are constant strain triangle elements, matching displacements at the nodes does not insure matching displacements along element sides. This is illustrated in the figure below.

Adjacent Finite Elements Before Loading

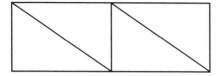

After Loading

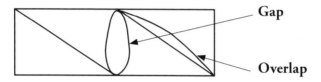

Note: Elements connected at nodes only

Figure 1.6 - <u>Deflected Constant Element Triangle Elements After Loading</u>

Figure 12 - <u>Discretization Error</u>

<u>Round-off Errors</u> – Errors because a computer uses a fixed number of digits while doing arithmetic.

There is no substitute for understanding both the problem you are trying to solve and the finite element model.

A simply supported cantiliver beam is shown below. The height of the beam is not small compared to the length. Thus the mechanics of materials, $\sigma = M y / I$, cannot be used. So the problem will be solved with finite element analysis.

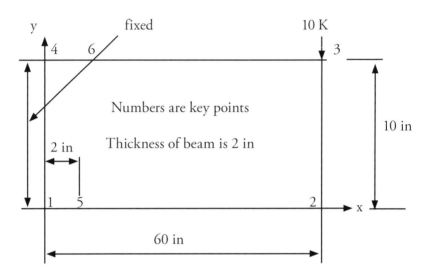

Figure 13 – Cantilever Deep Beam

The loads and boundary conditions for a mesh with constant strain triangle elements can only be applied at the nodes. Later in this book you will be shown how to convert a uniform load into a set of equivalent concentrated loads at the nodes. The constant strain triangle element is the only element that the stiffness matrix can be derived in closed form. It is a good element. It satisfies the convergence criteria. However you need too many elements to get an accurate solution.

There are two classes of two dimensional problems, plane stress and plain strain. In a plane stress problem, the thickness dimension is much smaller than the length and width dimensions. Plane strain problems model a long body. The geometry and loading do not change significantly in the longitudinal direction. Dams and retaining wall are examples of plain strain problems. The solution of plane strain problems does not apply to ends of the body.

The deep beam problem show on Figure 1.7 is a plane stress problem. The thickness of the beam is an input to the problem. A deep beam problem is Theory of Elasticity Problem. The mechanics of Materials equation, $\sigma = M\,y\,/\,I$, cannot be used to solve the problem. It must be solved numerically.

The Partial Differential Equation for 2-D Theory of Elasticity Problems is shown below.

$$\frac{\partial^4 \phi}{\partial x^4} + 2\frac{\partial^4 \phi}{\partial x^2 \partial y^2} + \frac{\partial^4 \phi}{\partial y^4} = 0$$

Φ is a stress function. The stresses are related to Φ.

$$\sigma_x = \frac{\partial^2 \phi_2}{\partial y^2} \qquad \sigma_y = \frac{\partial^2 \phi_2}{\partial x^2} ; \qquad \tau_{xy} = -\frac{\partial^2 \phi_2}{\partial x \partial y} ;$$

If the displacements are small compared to the dimensions of a domain of the problem, the compatibility equations are:

$\epsilon_x = \partial u/\partial x$

$\epsilon_y = \partial v/\partial y$

$\tau_{xy} = G \gamma_{xy}$

Hardy Cross's definition of compatibility was "If it doesn't pull apart, it sticks together. If the partial differential equation shown above and the boundary conditions are satisfied, the solution is unique. However do not forget that a finite element analysis solution is an exact solution to an approximate problem, your finite model.

Stress is related to strain with Hooke's law. For plane stress:

$\sigma = E/(1- \surd^2) (\epsilon_x + \surd \epsilon_y)$

$\sigma = E/(1- \surd^2) (\epsilon_y + \surd \epsilon_x)$

$$t_{xy} = G \, g_{xy}$$
$$G = E/2(1+\sqrt{\ })$$

Because the constant strain triangle is an element of constant strain and stress is proportional to strain, each element is an island of constant stress. Changes of stress are modeled by changes from element to element.

Example problems from my experience and the experiences of others will be presented in the following on line courses (sessions). References for some of the early finite element papers and books are listed below.

3

Original Finite Element Papers

1. "Stiffness and Deflection Analysis of Complex Structures", Turner, Clough, Martin, and Top, Journal of Aeronautical Sciences, 1956

2. "Energy Theorems and Structural Analysis", A Collection of Papers Published in the Aircraft Industry, 1954 and 1955.

3. "The Finite Element Method in Plane Stress Analysis", Clough, Ray, ASCE, 2nd Conference on Electric Computation, Pittsburgh, Pa. (1960)

Books

1. "Introduction to the Finite Element Method", A Numerical Method for Engineering Analysis, Chandrakant S.Desai and John F. Abel, Van Nostrand Reinhold Company, 1972_Company, 1972

2. "Concepts and Applications of Finite Element Analysis" 3rd Edition, Cook, Robert, Malkis, David S., Plesha, Michael E., John Wiley and Sons Inc, 1989

3. "Finite Element Modeling for Stress Analysis", Cook, Robert A., John Wiley and Sons Inc, 1995

My resume is shown below.

NAME   Dr. James A. Mandel P.E.   DATE   June 2021

Address: 7262 Leafcrest Lane
East Syracuse, N.Y. 13057
Telephone: (315) 656-2283
E-Mail: jmandel@twcny.rr.com

PERSONAL

Born: December 25, 1934, Pittsburgh, PA
Married to: Carolyn D. Mandel

EDUCATION

Degree	Date	Curriculum	University
B.S.	1956	Civil Engineering	Carnegie Institute of Technology
M.S.	1962	Civil Engineering	Carnegie Institute of Technology
Ph.D.	1967	Civil Engineering	Syracuse University

PhD. Dissertation: Stress Analysis of Translational Shells

ACADEMIC EMPLOYMENT

1966-1967   Instructor, Civil Engineering, Syracuse University

1967-1970   Assistant Professor, Civil Engineering, Syracuse University

| 1970-1978 | Associate Professor, Civil Engineering, Syracuse University |
| 1978-1996 | Professor, Civil Engineering, Syracuse University |

My duties included teaching, advising, and research.

The undergraduate courses I taught included:

Surveying, Photogrammetry, Mechanics of Materials, Structures I, Structures II, Transportation, Civil Engineering Systems, and the Senior Capstone Course.

The graduate Courses I taught included:

Structures, Design for Earthquake Loading, Plates and Shells, Theory of Elasticity, Reinforced Concrete Design, Structural Dynamics, Finite Element Analysis

1996-2014   Professor Emeritus, Civil Engineering, Syracuse University

Adjunct Professor, Civil Engineering, Syracuse University

Research Professor, Civil Engineering, Syracuse University

OTHER EMPLOYMENT

1956-1961   Design Engineering, Richardson, Gordon and Associates, Pittsburgh, PA

Designed many bridges, some on the interstate highway system, Highway route planning, and inspection.

8/3/57-   ARMY USAR CE, Released to USAR
12/13/57

1955   Bureau of Ships, U.S. Navy (Summer)

1961-1962   Swindler Dressler Corporation, Part-time

Taught bridge design to new employees

1962-1964   Senior Stress Engineer, Goodyear Aerospace Corp. Akron, Ohio

DR. JAMES A. MANDEL, P.E.

I worked on several projects at Goodyear Aerospace Corporation. The design of the Gemini Ballute was assigned to me.

The Gemini Ballute is deployed by the astronaut if he must eject from the capsule at Mach 2. A parachute will not open at Mach 2. The Ballute is a 48 inch diameter tear dropped drag device. It will stabilize the astronaut and reduce his speed until his parachute will open.

The ballute is a 48 diameter tear drop shaped drag device. It is stored in a small box on the backboard of the astronaut. When deployed it is filled with air through inlets.

I was responsible for the structural design of the Ballute, the design and testing of a shock absorber between the Ballute and the astronaut, and the wind tunnel testing of the Ballute.

Other members of the team were an aerodynamic engineer who computed the pressure loading on the Ballute, a packaging engineer, and a project engineer. A picture of the Ballute is on the cover of Aviation Week Space Technology,

The ballute is made fabric continuously reinforced with fabric straps in the meridional direction. The ballute stabilizes the astronaut. It prevents him from going into a flat spin. A flat spin would cause blood to go into his brain and kill him. A shock absorber is needed between the ballute and the astronaut's back-board, It is needed to prevent his shoulder from being torn off. The shock absorber could not be made of a metal.

After reviewing the stress-strain relationships of many materials, Mylar was chosen because it is nonmetallic, and it can absorb a lot of strain energy. The area under a stress strain diagram is the strain energy per unit volume that the material can absorb. A Mylar loop, approximately 6 inches long, was used as a shock absorber between the ballute and astronaut. There were many layers of mylar in the loop. Note: Mylar tape is Scotch Tape! A description of the testing of the shock absorber and the wind tunnel tests is given below. I was a scared young 29 year engineer.

DR. JAMES A. MANDEL, P.E.

TESTING THE MYLAR SHOCK ABSORBER

There is a cat walk 180 feet above the floor in the Goodyear Air Dock Building. The mylar shock absorber is attached to the cat walk. A wire is attached to the mylar shock. The wire is dropped. It stopped just above the floor of the Goodyear Air Dock Building. A stop is attached to end of the wire. A weight slides down the wire. It hits the stop creating a shock to the mylar shock absorber. A diagram of the test setup is shown below.

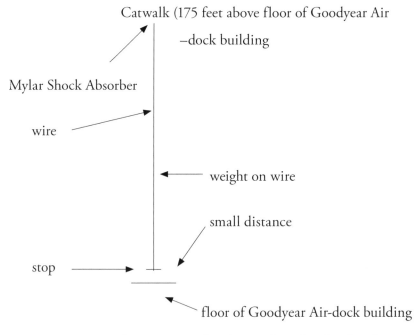

Diagram of Test Setup for the Mylar Shock Absorber

A grid was drawn on the Mylar shock absorber. A weight slid the wire. When it hit the stop, a shock load was applied to the Mylar shock absorber. The Mylar Shock Absorber was filmed with a high speed motion camera. By observing the grid frame by frame, the absorbed energy was calculated.

In the morning of the test, an elevator attendant took us to the catwalk. At noon he returned to take us down. While going down he screamed "The brakes failed we are going to die". He let the elevator go down quickly and then applied the brakes just before the elevator reached the concrete floor. That was his idea of a joke but it wasn't funny to me.

A 1/4th model of the ballute was tested in a wind tunnel. I did not go to the tests because my wife Rita was in her ninth month of pregnancy. I designed the structure to anchor the ballute in the wind tunnel. This structure is called a "sting". The wind tunnel is usually used to test airfoils, but the ballute is a drag device. This puts large stresses into the "sting". The "sting" is supposed to be as small as possible so it doesn't interfere with wind flow.

When the wind tunnel is turned on, a shock wave comes down the wind tunnel. If the natural frequency of the "sting" is close to the natural frequency of the shock wave, the "sting" will fail. It will hit the propellers of the wind tunnel, disabling the wind tunnel. The Gemini Ballute passed the wind tunnel tests.

The Gemini Capsule is in the Smithsonian Air Museum in Washington D.C.

I worked on several other projects at Goodyear Aerospace Corporation. They included the Polaris Missile Case. I developed an algorithm to model the stress-strain behavior of tire fabric. I also learned FORTRAN programming and wrote programs for my department.

CHAPTER 15 – <u>FELLOWSHIP AT SYRACUSE UNIVERSITY</u>

In 1966, Joey D and I went to a wedding in Cleveland Ohio. John V, a classmate of mine when I was studying for my Bachelor's Degree at Carnegie Institute of Technology was there. After graduation I worked for Richardson, Gordon, and Associates. Dr. V earned a PhD and was now an Assistant Professor at Syracuse University.

Dr. V offered me a fellowship to study for a PhD at Syracuse University. It paid all of the tuition and fees. In addition it paid me a stipend. I graduated in 1967. I was a full time professor in the Department of Civil and Environmental Engineering from 1967 until 2008. From 2008 to the present I taught part – time and performed research.

1966   Barton Brown Clyde Loguidice (Summer)

                    Designed a settling tank and a sludge digester

2004 – 2007   Performed research with the Radiology Department at Upstate Medical Center. Developed technique and software for registration of 3-D breast images (MRI/PET).

                    This technique was successful in a breast cancer patient study.

2014 – Present   Research on the Structural Analysis of Aircraft and Drones and Composite Materials (CEO – Dr. James A. Mandel P.E. dba Airfoil Analytics)

PROFESSIONAL SPECIALIZATION

Fracture mechanics

Finite element analysis

Analytical and experimental studies in plates and shells

Response of structures to short pulse-type loading

Methods of numerical analysis in civil engineering

Intermodality non-rigid breast registration

AWARDS

The Dr. James A. Mandel Prize for Achievement in Civil and Environmental Engineering was established in April 2006 to be given annually to an outstanding Civil Engineering graduate who is a member of the National Society of Black Engineers. This endowment was established at Syracuse University by five of my former students.

Dr. James A. Mandel and Samuel Clemence DCC – Syracuse University Internship Program. Established in 2009 by the Dubai Construction Company.

RESEARCH GRANTS

"Analytical and experimental studies of castellated beams," New York state Department of Public Works, 1967-1968.

"Analysis of structures subjected to high energy loadings," Syracuse University Research Institute, 1968-1969.

"Transmission of flexural and longitudinal stress waves in rigid frame structures," National Science Foundation, 1969-1970.

"Fracture mechanics of fibrous composite materials," National Science Foundation, 1978-1980.

"Fracture mechanics of fibrous composite materials," National Science Foundation, 1980-1982.

"The effect of soil embedment on the seismic analysis of structures founded on rock," Niagara Mohawk Power Corporation, 1981-1982.

"Micromechanical studies of crack growth in fiber reinforced cementitious materials," National Science Foundation, 1983-1986.

PUBLICATIONS

Refereed Journal Articles

Romaldi, J.P. and J.A. Mandel. 1964. "Crack arrest in concrete with randomly distributed short wire reinforcement," *Journal of the American Concrete Institute,* June.

Li, W.H., B.M. Tang, and J.A. Mandel. 1967. "Symmetrical vibration of a thick circular membrane," *Journal of Applied Mechanics,* December.

Mandel, J.A., and P.J. Brennan. 1968. "Stress analysis of translational shells," *Journal of the Engineering Mechanics Division,* American Society of Civil Engineering, October

Mandel, J.A., P.J. Brennan, B.A. Wasil, and C.M. Antoni. 1971. "Stress distribution in castellated beams," *Journal of the Structural Division,* American Society of Civil Engineers, July.

Mandel, J.A., F.K. Mathur, and Y.C. Chang. 1971. "Stress waves at a rigid angle joint," *Journal of the Engineering Mechanics Division,* American Society of Civil Engineers, August.

Brennan, P.J. and J.A. Mandel. 1975. "User manual-Program for three dimensional analysis of horizontally curved bridges," Federal Highway Administration, U.S. Department of Transportation, August.

Brennan, P.J., and J.A. Mandel. 1975. "Analysis of small scale structure ramp-over Interstate 1290 Springfield, MA, through three dimensional mathematical method and structural testing," Federal Highway Administration, U.S. Department of Transportation, August.

Brennan, P.J., and J.A. Mandel. 1975. "Analysis and structural testing of a multiple configuration small scale horizontally curved highway bridge," Federal Highway Administration, U.S. Department of Transportation, August.

Brennan, P.J., J.A. Mandel, C.M. Antoni, and R. Leininger. 1975. "Analysis of horizontally curved girder bridges through three dimensional mathematical method and small structural testing," Federal Highway Administration, U.S. Department of Transportation, August.

Brennan, P.J., and J.A. Mandel. 1975. "Analysis of Seekonk River bridge small scale structure through three dimensional mathematical method and structural testing," Federal Highway Administration, U.S. Department of Transportation, August.

Brennan, P.J., J.A. Mandel, C.M. Antoni, and R. Leininger. 1976. "Analysis of horizontally curved girder bridge through a geometric scale model," *T5ransportation Research Board 607,* Transportation Research Board, National Academy of Science.

Brennan, P.J., and J.A. Mandel. 1978. "Curved girder bridge model analysis and testing," *International Association for Bridge and Structural Engineering,* November.

Brennan, P.J., and J.A. Mandel. 1979. "Multiple configuration curved bridge model studies," *Journal of Structural Division, American Society of Civil Engineers,* May.

Mandel, J.A., and S.C. Pack. 1982. "Crack growth in fiber reinforced materials," *Journal of the Engineering Mechanics Division,* American Society of Civil Engineers, June.

Mandel, J.A., S.C. Pack, and S. Tarazi. 1982. "Micromechanical studies of crack growth in fiber reinforced materials," *Engineering Fracture Mechanics,* 16(5).

Mandel, J.A., and R.M. Bakeer. 1983. "Simplified finite element mesh for dynamic analysis of a nuclear reactor building," *International Journal for Numerical Methods in Engineering,* 19:1403-1420.

Brennan, P.J., and J.A. Mandel. 1983. "Load capacity for arch bridge rehabilitation," *Journal of Civil Engineering for Practicing and Design Engineers,* Pergamon Press, Elmsford Park, NY, Vol. 2.

Pack, S.C., and J.A. Mandel. 1984. "2-D multiplane finite element technique for solving a class of 3-D problems,"

International Journal for Numerical Methods in Engineering, 19:113-124.

Pack, S.C., and J.A. Mandel. 1984. "Micromechanical multiplane finite element modeling of crack growth in fiber reinforced materials," *Engineering Fracture Mechanics,* 20(2):335-349.

Pack, S.C., and J.A. Mandel. 1986. "An improved finite element for connecting adjacent laminal of 2D elements," *International Journal for Numerical Methods in Engineering,* Vol. 23.

Wei, S., J.A. Mandel, and S. Said. 1986. "Study of the interface strength in steel fiber reinforced cement-based composites," *Journal of the American Concrete Institute,* 83(4).

Mandel, J.A., S. Wei, and S. Said. 1987. "Studies of the properties of the fiber-matrix interface in steel fiber reinforced mortar," *ACI Materials Journal,* 84(2).

Tarazi, S., and J.A. Mandel. 1988. "Zero thickness quarter point crack tip element for modeling an interface between two materials," *Engineering Fracture Mechanics,* 30(1).

Said, S., and J.A. Mandel. 1989. "Micromechanical studies of crack growth in steel fiber reinforced mortar," *ACI Materials Journal*, 86(3).

Mandel, J.A. and S. Said. 1990. "Effect of the addition of acrylic polymer on the mechanical properties of mortar," *ACI Materials Journal*, 87(1):54-61.

Tarazi, S., and J.A. Mandel. 1990. "A numerical technique for the solution of two dimensional elasticity problems," *International Journal for Numerical Methods in Engineering*, 29:1759-1785.

Siah, K., J.A. Mandel, and B.R. Mousa. 1992. "A micromechanical finite element model for fiber reinforced cementitious materials," *ACI Materials Journal*, 89(3):277-288.

Unlu, M, Krol, A, Coman, I, Mandel, J Baum, K, Lee, W, Lipson, E, Feighlin, D., "Implementation of Deformable Breast Model for 3D Nonrigid Breast Image Registration In F-18- FDG Dynamic Pet Studies", Eur. J. Nuc. Med., 32, S77, 2005

Unlu, M, Krol, A, Feighlin, D, Mandel, J. Lee, W, Coman, I, Lipson, E, " Fusion of F-18-FDG Pet and MR Mammography via Nonrigid Breast-Image Registration", Eur. J. Nuc. Med., 32, S77, 2005

Krol, A, Feighlin, D, Unlu, M, Mandel, J, Magri, A, Lee, W, Coman, I, Lipson, E, "New Approach to F-18-FDG Pet Dynamic Data Acquisition and Analysis for Breast Cancer Imaging", Eur. J. Nuc. Med., 32, S150, 2005

Krol, A, Unlu, M, Baum, K, Mandel, J, Lee, W Coman, I, Lipson,E, Feighlin, D, "MRI/PET Nonrigid Breast Registration Using Fiducial Skin Markers", Physica Medica (European Journal of Medical Physics), Vol XXI, Supplement 1, 31-35, 2006

Lipson, E, Krol,A, Unlu, M, Coman, I, Mandel, J, Lee, W, Feighlin, D, "Development of Defomable Model for 3D Nonrigid Breast Image Registration for Improved Breast Cancer Diagnosis", Int. J. Sci. Res., 16:291-296, 2006

Magri, A., Krol, A., Unlu, D.H., Lipson, E., Mandel, J., McGraw, W., Lee, W., Coman, I.O., Feiglin, D. "Nonrigid

DR. JAMES A. MANDEL, P.E.

Registration of Dynamic Breast F-18-FDG PET/CD Images using Deformable FEM Model and CT Image Warping", Proc. SPIE Vol. 6512 Medical Imaging 2007: Image Processing, 651212, 2007

Krol,A., Magri, A., Unlu, M., Feiglin, D., Lipson, E., Mandel, J., Tillapough-Fay, G., Lee, W., Coman, I., Szeverenya, N.M., "Motion Correction Via Nonrigid Coregistration of Dynamic MR Mammography Series" Proc. SPIE Vol. 6144, 614439 Medical Imaging 2006: Image Processing

Unlu, M.Z., Krol, A., Magri, A., Mandel, J.A., Lee, W., Baum, K.G., Lipson,E., Coman, I.L., Feiglin, D.H. "Computerized Method for Nonrigid MR-to-Pet Breast-Image Registration" Computers in Biology and Medicine, 40 (2010) 37-53

CONFERENCE PROCEEDINGS

Brennan, P.J., Mandel, J.A., "Stress Amplification and Buckling in Arch Ribs", Annual Technical Session of the Column Research Council Lehigh University Bethlehem, Pa., April 6,1966

Brock, R.H., B.A. Wasil and J.A. Mandel, "Three station analytic photogrammetry for stress analysis of a plate with large displacements," *Symposium on "Close Range Photogrammetry,* Urbana, IL, January 26. 1971

Gabriel, J.R., J.A. Mandel, and E.J. Haggerty. 1981. "The application of lightweight modular structures to housing," *International Conference on Housing,* Vienna, Austria, Nov. 15-18.

Gabriel, J.R., and J.A. Mandel. 1984. "A space-frame building system for housing," *Third International Conference on Space Structures*, Elsevier Applied Science Publishers, October.

Mandel, J.A. 1985. "Micromechanical modeling of steel fiber reinforced cementitious materials," *U.S.-Sweden Joint Seminar on Steel Fiber Concrete*, Stockholm, Sweden.

Brennan, P.J., and J.A. Mandel. 1989. "Load path control in the design and rehabilitation of girder bridges," *6th Annual Bridge Conference and Exhibition*, Pittsburg, PA, June 12-14.

Coman, I.O., M. Luo, D. H. Feiglin, J.A. Mandel, E.D. Lipson, J. Beaumont. "Multimodality Image Fusion for Enhanced Breast Cancer Diagnosis", Eur. J. Nuc. Med. 30, S330-S331 (2003).

Bansal, M., Kornreich, P., Negussey, D., Flattery, J., Mandel, J., " Strain and Sonar Detection with Lithium Coated Core Fiber", Defense, Security, Sensing and SPIE Conference, Orlando Fl. April 2010

A. Krol, I.L. Coman, J. Mandel, K, Baum, M. Luo, D.H. Feiglin, E.D. Lipson, J. Beaumont, "Inter-modality non-rigid breast image registration using Finite-Element Method", IEEE Nuclear Science Symposium and Medical Imaging Conference Record (2003).

I.L. Coman, A. Kroll, J.A. Mandel, K.G. Baum, M. Luo, E.D. Lipson, D.H. Feiglin, "Finite-Element Method for intermodality non-rigid breast registration using external skin markers", Proceedings of SPIE, 5370 (2004).

I. Coman, A. Krol, D. Feiglin, W. Li, E. Lipson, J. Mandel, K. Baum, M. Unlu, Li, W. "Intermodality Nonrigid Breast-Image Registration", Proceedings of IEEE International Symposium on Biomedical Imaging, ISBI 2004 From Nano to Macro, pp. 1439-1442 (2004)

SOFTWARE

CBRIDGE: Three Dimensional Horizontally Curved Bridge Analysis Program (with P.J. Brennan) completed with software development and User Manual, marketed by Telos Software, Inc.

Registration of MRI and PET scans of breast cancer patients using ANSYS finite element software and for the radiology department of Upstate Medical University

Finite Element Software for the Structural Analysis of Aircraft and Drones Finite Element Software for Computing the Tensile Strength and Fracture Toughness of Composite Materials (copywrite TxU002192438)

TECHNICAL ACHIEVEMENTS

Structural design of the the GEMINI BALLUTE – on the cover of Aviation Week, April 6, 1964 – in the Smithsonian Institute.

Developed an online course and E-Book for "Finite Element Analysis", Syracuse University 2015

INVITED PRESENTATIONS

Invited lecturer to Nanjing Institute of Technology, Nanjing, Jiangsu, Peoples Republic of China, June 1985. (Sponsored by the Ministry of Education of the Peoples Republic of China and the National Science Foundation of the United States of America).

SERVICE

College and Departmental Committees

Professional Registration

Registered Professional Engineer in Pennsylvania

Consulting Activities

Franklin Steel Corporation – Analysis of post sections.

Moravia School District – Settlement of an elementary school (with Louis Goodman).

Cambridge Filter Company – Analysis and testing of filter bank units for vibration and strength (with Paul J. Brennan).

Syracuse University (Physical Plant) – Investigation of anchorage requirements and temperature stress in pipe loops.

Syracuse University Research Corporation – Evaluation of structural analysis procedures for LFV Microwave Towers (with Paul J. Brennan).

Temple Beth El – Settlement studies of the main sanctuary (unpaid).

Holy Family Catholic Church – Problems with school building (unpaid), (with Samuel Clemence).

Barton and Loguidice, P.C. – Structural investigation and evaluation of a reinforced concrete arch highway bridge (with Paul J. Brennan).

Charles T. Driscoll Masonry Restoration Co., Inc. – Deck sealant failures in Parking Garages and studies of the safety reinforced concrete composite roof beams.

Plumley Engineering P.C. – Check on the accuracy of the structural analysis of the Woodhill Creek Railroad bridge.

Upstate Medical University – Radiology Department – Registration of MRI and PET scans of breast cancer patients. (unpaid)

Charles T. Driscoll Masonry Restoration Co., Inc – Failure in water tanks

University Hospital – Investigation of failure in slab on grade foundation

Printed in the United States
by Baker & Taylor Publisher Services